GET READY TO WRITE

A BEGINNING WRITING TEXT

KAREN BLANCHARD
CHRISTINE ROOT

Longman

This book is dedicated to our families, friends, colleagues, and students for their help beyond all measuring.

Acknowledgments

We are grateful to Jeff Diluglio, John Dumicich, Carolyn Graham, Jane Sloan, and Robby Steinberg for helping us keep the purpose of this text in focus. We would also like to express our appreciation to Allen Ascher, Janet Aitchison, Christine Cervoni, Amy Durfy, and Françoise Leffler at Addison Wesley Longman for their unfailing support.

Get Ready to Write: A Beginning Writing Text

Pearson Education, 10 Bank Street, White Plains, NY 10606-1951

Acquisitions editor: Janet Aitchison
Development editor: Françoise Leffler
Production editor: Christine Cervoni
Photo research: Amy Durfy
Cover design adaptation: Naomi Ganor
Text design adaptation: Kathleen Marks
Electronic production supervisor: Kim Teixeira
Text composition: Kim Teixeira, Kathleen Marks
Text art: Tom Sperling
Text credits: p. 61, three Haiku poems by Vasakorn Bhadranavik, Kazu Karasawa, Fumihiko Suita. Published in *Class Books of Robby Steinberg* 1993–1996. Reprinted by permission of Robby Steinberg; p. 89, Using Poetry to Write about Memories and Writing Your Memory Poem—source: *Singing, Chanting, Telling Tales, Arts in the Language Classroom* by Carolyn Graham. Printed with special thanks to Carolyn Graham.

Grateful acknowledgment is given to the following for providing illustrations and photographs: p. 16, © Bob Daemmrich/The Image Works; p. 22, printed by permission of the Norman Rockwell Family Trust. Copyright © 1960 the Norman Rockwell Family Trust. Photo courtesy of the Archives of the American Illustrators Gallery, New York City; p. 31, Marriott International, Washington, D.C.; p. 45, Smithsonian Institution Air & Space Museum; p. 46, © Michael Lutch; p. 47, Fernando Medina/© NBA Photos. All rights reserved; p. 49, © Luis Miguel Palomares; p. 49, International Tennis Hall of Fame & Museum, Newport, RI; p. 58, photo by Ramona Boudreau. Courtesy of Flagstaff Convention & Visitors Bureau; p. 61, reprinted by permission of Robby Steinberg; p. 90, UPI/Corbis-Bettman

Library of Congress Cataloging–in–Publication Data
Blanchard, Karen Lourie.
    Get ready to write: a beginning writing text/Karen Blanchard, Christine Root.
      p.   cm.
    ISBN 0–201–69517–0
    1. English language—Textbooks for foreign speakers. 2. English language—Rhetoric—Problems, exercises, etc. 3. Report writing—Problems, exercises, etc.
    I. Root, Christine Baker, II. Title.
PE 1128.B5865 1998
808 ' .042—dc21   97–7382
                                                          CIP

7 8 9 10—ML—04 03 02 01

Contents

Introduction

Get Ready to Write is a beginning-level writing skills textbook for students of English as a Second Language who have some limited knowledge of both written and spoken English. *Get Ready to Write* is designed to acquaint students with the basic skills required for good writing and to help them become comfortable, confident, and independent writers in English.

Although it is a writing text, *Get Ready to Write* integrates reading, speaking, and listening skills with prewriting, planning, and rewriting. As in *Ready to Write* and *Ready to Write More,* students are called upon to write frequently and on a broad range of topics. *Get Ready to Write* is based on the premise that students at this level can and want to express themselves in English. What they need in order to do so effectively is an ever-expanding vocabulary base and successive opportunities to write short, confidence-building pieces.

It is our intention in *Get Ready to Write* to introduce, without being overly didactic, the basic skills required for good writing in English. Through an abundance of pair and group activities as well as individual writing tasks, students learn the fundamental principles of prewriting, planning, drafting, revising, and editing as they move from sentence-level writing to guided paragraphs and beyond. We believe that having students write early and often instills in them the confidence necessary for successful writing.

Two popular features of *Ready to Write* and *Ready to Write More,* "On Your Own" and "You Be the Editor," appear in every chapter throughout *Get Ready to Write.* "On Your Own" provides students with further, less structured practice. "You Be the Editor" provides practice in error correction and editing to help students monitor their own errors. The errors have all been modeled in some way within the chapter or in a previous chapter of the book. An Answer Key is included at the back of the book for these exercises.

A new feature is the inclusion of "Word Banks," which supply students with useful, pertinent vocabulary and the opportunity to try out the new words in their writing.

Another new feature is the "Autobiography" that students will assemble at the back of the book. This autobiography will be made up of autobiographical paragraphs, letters, poems, and drawings that students will be asked to produce throughout the course. The autobiographical entries include the following:

- Cover design (p. 2)
- To Introduce Myself (p. 4)
- The Things I Like to Do (p. 6)
- My Family Tree (p. 11)
- My Family (p. 13)
- My Best Friend (p. 15)
- My Daily Activities (p. 22)
- My Favorite Holiday (p. 24)
- My Favorite Hobbies (p. 27)
- What I Do to Stay Healthy (p. 36)
- What I Look Like (p. 42)
- The Way I Am (p. 44)
- My Home (p. 54)
- My Hometown (p. 59)
- My Haiku (p. 62)
- My Dream Car (p. 71)
- My Finished Story (p. 87)
- My Memory Poem (p. 89)
- A Memory from My Childhood (p. 90)

At the end of the course, students will be asked to share their autobiographies with their classmates.

We hope that you and your students enjoy the activities in this text as they *get ready to write.*

KLB and CBR

Writing about Yourself

Learning to write in a new language is not always easy. It is challenging, but it can also be fun. If you are learning to speak and read in a new language, you are ready to begin writing too.

The easiest way to begin writing is to write about things you know well. That often means writing about yourself.

Getting Ready to Write about Yourself

A story you write about yourself is called an *autobiography*. In many ways, doing the exercises in this book will be like writing your autobiography. In fact, there is a special "Autobiography" section at the back of this book (pp. 97–107) where you will be able to paste the autobiographical paragraphs, letters, poems, and drawings that you will produce throughout the course.

A. An autobiography starts with its cover. Look at the cover that a student designed for his autobiography.

B. Design the cover for your own autobiography. Do it on a separate piece of paper. Use drawings, pictures, and words to describe who you are. Here are some suggestions for things to include:

- Your family and friends
- Your interests and hobbies
- Sports you like to play or watch
- Your job, profession, or major in school
- Your favorite places, foods, holidays, activities

C. Paste your design on the front page of your autobiography (p. 97).

Introducing Yourself

Introduce yourself to your classmates. Here are some suggestions:

- Show and explain the cover of your autobiography.
- Write your name on the chalkboard and teach your classmates how to pronounce it.
- If your name has a special meaning, explain it to the class.
- Tell your classmates why you are studying English.

Answering a Questionnaire about Yourself

A. Answer these questions about yourself in one or two words.

1. What is your name? _____

2. How old are you? _____

3. Where are you from? _____

4. What is your native language? _____

5. What are some things you like to do? _____

_____

_____

6. What do you do? (Are you a student? Are you a businessperson?

Are you a secretary? lawyer? musician?) _____

_____

B. Use your answers to complete each of the following sentences. Then copy the complete sentence on the line.

EXAMPLE: My name is <u>Isabela Fernandez</u>.

    <u>My name is Isabela Fernandez.</u>

1. My name is _____.

   _____

2. I am _____ years old.

   _____

3. I am from _____.

   _____

4. My native language is _____.

   _____

5. I like _____.

   _____

6. I am a _____.

   _____

Getting Ready to Write a Paragraph

What is a paragraph?

A paragraph is a group of sentences about one main idea. This main idea is called the *topic*.

What does a paragraph look like?

An English paragraph has a special form. Look at the paragraph below. It is written in the correct form.

> *My name is Christine Baker. I am 32 years old. I am from Boston, Massachusetts. My native language is English. I am an author and a teacher.*

Keep the following rules in mind when you write your paragraph.

👉 **Paragraph Pointers: Rules of Paragraph Writing**

---

1. Indent the first word of a new paragraph.
2. Begin each sentence with a capital letter.
3. End each sentence with a period.
4. Do not start each new sentence on a new line.

What is wrong with this paragraph?

A. The following paragraph is not written in the correct form. Look at the paragraph with a partner and discuss what is wrong with the form.

my name is Karen Lowrie

i am 30 years old

i am from Philadelphia, Pennsylvania

my native language is English

i am a fashion designer

B. Now copy the paragraph correctly on the lines below.

Writing a Paragraph about Yourself

Use the sentences you wrote about yourself on page 3 to write a short paragraph. Be sure to follow the rules of paragraph writing. Write your paragraph on a separate piece of paper. After your teacher has checked your paragraph, copy it over, and paste it in your autobiography (p. 98) under the title "To Introduce Myself."

Filling Out a Form

Fill out the form below with information about yourself.

Edge Hill College English Program

Please Print

1. Name: Mr.
   Mrs. _____
   Ms.   Last   First   Middle

2. Local Address: _____

   _____

3. Phone Number: _____

4. Nationality: _____

5. Native Language: _____

6. Other Languages: _____

7. How long have you studied English? *(Please check one)*

   _____ Never

   _____ Less than 1 year

   _____ 1–2 years

   _____ More than 2 years

8. Which term do you plan to enroll for? *(Please check one)*

   _____ Fall

   _____ Winter

   _____ Spring

   _____ Summer

9. Do you plan to be a full-time or a part-time student? *(Please check one)*

   _____ Full-time

   _____ Part-time

10. Signature: _____

Writing a Paragraph about What You Like to Do

A. Answer the following questions about yourself. Use the word bank to help you with vocabulary.

Word Bank			
bake	go to museums	play golf	sew
cook	go to parties	play guitar	sing
dance	go to the movies	play piano	ski
draw	knit	play soccer	swim
exercise	listen to music	play tennis	travel
go shopping	paint	read	watch TV

Page 1

1. What do you like to do in your free time? Make a list.

_____   _____

_____   _____

_____   _____

2. What are some things you want to learn how to do? Make a list.

_____   _____

_____   _____

B. Write a short paragraph about the things you like to do. Use a separate piece of paper. After your teacher has checked your paragraph, copy it over, and paste it in your autobiography (p. 98) under the title "The Things I Like to Do."

Writing about a Classmate

A. Ask one of your classmates the following questions. Write the answers on the lines.

1. What is your name? _____

2. How old are you? _____

3. Are you married or single? _____

4. Where are you from? _____

5. What is your native language? _____

6. What do you do? (Are you a student? Are you a businessperson?

   Are you a secretary? lawyer? musician?) _____

7. What are your hobbies? _____

   _____

B. Use your answers to complete each of the following sentences about your classmate. Then copy the complete sentence on the line.

EXAMPLE: My classmate's name is _Oscar_____ .

   _My classmate's name is Oscar._____

1. My classmate's name is _____ .

   _____

2. He/She is _____ years old.

   _____

3. He/She is _____ .

   _____

4. He/She is from _____ .

   _____

5. His/Her native language is _____ .

   _____

6. He/She is a _____ .

   _____

7. His/Her hobbies are _____ .

   _____

C. Use your sentences to write a short paragraph about your classmate. Remember to follow the rules of paragraph writing.

   _____

   _____

   _____

   _____

   _____

   _____

Ready to Write

On Your Own

A. Complete this fact sheet about Matthew Simmons. Use the information from the cover of his autobiography on page 1.

Name:	
Age:	
Hobbies:	
Sports:	
Music:	
Major:	

B. Now, write a paragraph about Matthew Simmons.

_____

_____

_____

_____

_____

_____

_____

C. Exchange paragraphs with a partner. Read your partner's paragraph and check *yes* or *no* for each question on the Peer Review Checklist below. Then help your partner improve his/her paragraph.

Peer Review Checklist		
	YES	NO
1. Is the first word of the paragraph indented?	☐	☐
2. Does each sentence begin with a capital letter?	☐	☐
3. Does each sentence end with a period?	☐	☐
4. Does each new sentence begin next to the one before it?	☐	☐

 **You Be the Editor**

A. Read this paragraph. It contains five mistakes. With a partner, find the five mistakes and correct them.

My name is Stanley Stoico.

I am 90 years old. I was born in Ravenna, Italy, and lived there until I was 9 years old. Then I moved to New York with my parents and my three older brothers. in my younger years I had many different jobs. I worked hard and saved my money By 1945 I had saved enough money to start my own retail business. The business was successful, and I retired in 1973. my hobbies are studying the stock market and playing golf. I have seen and done a lot in my long life I am a lucky and happy man.

B. Copy your corrected paragraph on the lines below.
Then check your work in the Answer Key on page 93.

_____

_____

_____

_____

_____

_____

_____

_____

CHAPTER 2

Writing about Your Family and Friends

Getting Ready to Write about Your Family

A. Discuss the meanings of the words in the word bank below with your teacher and classmates.

Word Bank

mother	father	mother-in-law	father-in-law
daughter	son	daughter-in-law	son-in-law
grandmother	grandfather	stepmother	stepfather
granddaughter	grandson	stepdaughter	stepson
great-grandmother	great-grandfather	sister	brother
great-granddaughter	great-grandson	aunt	uncle
child/children	parents	niece	nephew

Page 1

B. Look at Scott Solomon's family tree on the next page and answer these questions.

1. What is Scott's sister's name? _____

2. Who are Scott's parents? _____

3. How many cousins does Scott have? _____

4. How many grandsons do Stuart and Tammy have? _____

5. Who is Connie's daughter? _____

6. What are the names of Scott's uncles? _____

7. Who are Donna's brothers-in-law? _____

8. Who is Steve's mother-in-law? _____

9. Who are Scott's grandparents? _____

10. How many nephews does Richard have? _____

C. On a separate piece of paper, draw your own family tree.
When you are finished, paste it in your autobiography (p. 99) under the title "My Family Tree."

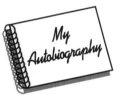

Writing about Your Family

A. Answer these questions about your family in complete sentences.

EXAMPLE: How many people are there in your family?

> *There are four people in my family.*

1. How many people are there in your family?

_____

2. What is your father's name?

_____

3. How old is your father?

_____

4. What is your mother's name?

_____

5. How old is your mother?

_____

6. Where do your parents live?

_____

7. What does your father do?

_____

8. What does your mother do?

_____

9. How many brothers do you have?

_____

10. What are their names?

_____

11. How old are they?

_____

12. How many sisters do you have?

_____

13. What are their names?

_____

14. How old are they?

_____

15. Are you married or single?

_____

16. Do you have any children? How many?

_____

17. What are their names?

_____

18. How old are they?

_____

B. Now use some of your sentences to write a short paragraph about your family. Remember to follow the rules of paragraph writing. Write your paragraph on a separate piece of paper. After your teacher has checked your paragraph, copy it over, and paste it in your autobiography (p. 99) under the title "My Family."

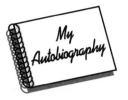

Writing about a Family Member

Complete the following steps.

A. Choose someone in your family to write about.

Write his/her name here. _____

B. Fill in the following information about your relative.

1. How is this person related to you? _____

2. How old is he/she? _____

3. Is he/she married or single? _____

4. Where does he/she live? _____

5. What does he/she do? _____

6. What are his/her hobbies? _____

C. Add one or two other interesting facts about your relative.

_____

_____

D. Write a paragraph about your relative. Use as much information as you want. Include your relative's name in the first sentence.

_____

_____

_____

_____

_____

_____

_____

_____

_____

On Your Own

A. What are some things that your family does together?
Make a list.

_____

_____

_____

_____

_____

B. Use your list to finish the following paragraph.

My family likes to do many things together. _____

_____

_____

_____

_____

_____

_____

_____

_____

_____

C. Exchange paragraphs with a partner. Read your partner's paragraph and check *yes* or *no* to each question on the Peer Review Checklist. Then help your partner improve his/her paragraph.

Peer Review Checklist		
	YES	NO
1. Is the first word of the paragraph indented?	☐	☐
2. Does each sentence begin with a capital letter?	☐	☐
3. Does each sentence end with a period?	☐	☐
4. Does each new sentence begin next to the one before it?	☐	☐

Getting Ready to Write about Friends

A. In small groups, discuss the qualities of a good friend.
Put a check next to the qualities that you think are important.

1. _____ responsible   6. _____ honest

2. _____ fun to be with   7. _____ good-looking

3. _____ kind   8. _____ wealthy

4. _____ intelligent   9. _____ loyal

5. _____ good listener   10. _____ warm

B. Describe your best friend to the people in your group.

Writing about a Friend

Complete the following steps.

A. Choose a friend that you would like to write about.

Write his/her name here. _____

B. Fill in the following information about your friend.

1. How old is he/she? _____

2. Is he/she married or single? _____

3. Where does he/she live? _____

4. What does he/she do? _____

5. What are his/her hobbies? _____

6. What are his/her qualities? _____

C. Add one or two more interesting facts about your friend.

_____

_____

D. Write a paragraph about your friend. Use as much information as you want. Write your paragraph on a separate piece of paper. After your teacher has checked your paragraph, copy it over, and paste it in your autobiography (p. 100) under the title "My Best Friend."

Use Your Imagination

A. Look at the following photograph.

B. With your classmates, discuss answers to the following questions.

    1. Where do you think this photograph was taken?

    2. Who are these people? Do you think they are family, friends, or co-workers?

    3. What do you think they are doing?

C. In small groups, work together to make up a story about the people in the photograph. Use the questions above to help you get started.

On Your Own

A. What are some things that you like to do with your friends? Make a list.

_____

_____

_____

_____

_____

B. Use your list to finish the following paragraph.

I enjoy spending time with my friends. _____

_____

_____

_____

_____

_____

_____

_____

C. Exchange paragraphs with a partner. Read your partner's paragraph and check *yes* or *no* to each question on the Peer Review Checklist. Then help your partner improve his/her paragraph.

Peer Review Checklist	YES	NO
1. Is the first word of the paragraph indented?	☐	☐
2. Does each sentence begin with a capital letter?	☐	☐
3. Does each sentence end with a period?	☐	☐
4. Does each new sentence begin next to the one before it?	☐	☐

 Be the Editor

A. Read this paragraph. It contains five mistakes. With a partner, find the five mistakes and correct them.

My cousin's name is Bettina Lee.

She is 37 years old. she was born in Chicago, Illinois, but now She lives in Denver, Colorado. She is married and has two children. Bettina is a beautiful ice-skater She used to skate professionally in ice shows when she was single. now she teaches ice-skating to young children.

B. Copy your corrected paragraph on the lines below. Then check your work in the Answer Key on page 93.

_____

_____

_____

_____

_____

_____

_____

Writing about Daily Activities

Getting Ready to Write about Daily Activities

Look at the eight pictures below. They describe a typical day in the life of a man named Roberto Trevino.

- Find the sentence that goes with each picture from the list on the next page.
- Write that sentence on the lines under the picture.

1. _____

2. _____

3. _____

4. _____

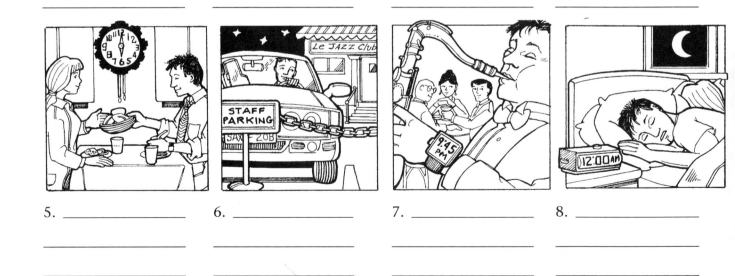

5. _____

6. _____

7. _____

8. _____

a. He teaches his class from 8:30 to 3:30.

b. First of all, Roberto gets up at seven o'clock every morning.

c. Roberto is exhausted when he gets into bed at midnight.

d. He always takes the 7:45 A.M. train to the elementary school where he works.

e. At six o'clock he eats dinner and gets ready for his night job.

f. Then he takes the 4:00 P.M. train back home.

g. He plays the saxophone from 8:00 to 11:00 P.M.

h. After dinner Roberto drives to a jazz club where he plays in a band.

Paragraph Practice

Use the sentences from the previous activity to complete a paragraph about a typical day in Roberto's life.

Roberto's days are very busy because he has two jobs.

_____

_____

_____

_____

_____

_____

Roberto has a very active life.

☞ **Paragraph Pointers: Time Order**

When you write a paragraph about daily activities, you should put your sentences in time order. To show time relationships, you will need to use **signal words.** These words help guide your reader from one idea to the next.

Here are some common signal words used to show time order:

first

second

next

then

finally

Practicing Time Order

The following sentences belong to the same paragraph, but they are not in the correct order.

Read the sentences and put them in the correct time order.
Write a *1* in front of the sentence you think should be first, and so on. Then write the sentences in paragraph form.

A. ____ Then he quickly gets dressed and eats breakfast.

   1 Mehmet's mornings are very busy.

   ____ At 7:45 he is outside waiting for the school bus.

   ____ His mother wakes him up at 6:30.

_____

_____

_____

B. ____ She spends the morning working out at the gym.

   ____ Finally, she works at a store from 5:00 to 9:00 P.M.

   ____ Then she takes classes at the university in the afternoon.

   ____ Maria is very active during the summer.

_____

_____

_____

C. ____ At 6:00 A.M. he goes to the flower market.

   ____ Mr. Park owns a busy flower shop.

   ____ Then he works in his shop from 9:00 to 4:00.

   ____ In the late afternoon he delivers flowers.

_____

_____

_____

_____

Writing about Your Daily Activities

A. Study the words and phrases in the word bank with your classmates and teacher. Then add several more words or phrases of your own to share with your class.

Word Bank			
wake up	get up	take a shower	take a bath
shave	put on makeup	get dressed	make the bed
make breakfast/lunch/dinner	go to school	go to work	do the dishes
do the laundry	do homework	get undressed	get ready for bed
go to bed			

Page 1

B. In the boxes below, draw simple pictures that show what you do on a typical weekday. Write a sentence to go with each picture. The first one has been done for you. Change the time to make it true for you.

1.   _I wake up at_
7:00 every morning.
_____

2. _____
_____
_____

3. _____
_____
_____

4. _____
_____
_____

5. _____
_____
_____

6. _____
_____
_____

7. _____
_____
_____

8. _____
_____
_____

C. Use your sentences to write a paragraph about a typical day in your life. Complete the following sentence and use it as the first sentence of your paragraph.

During the week, my days are very _____

(busy/boring/interesting/relaxed).

Write your paragraph on a separate piece of paper. After your teacher has checked your paragraph, copy it over, and paste it in your autobiography (p. 100) under the title "My Daily Activities."

Use Your Imagination

A. The picture below is called "The Window Washer."

Discuss the picture in small groups. Here are some questions to help you get started.

1. What do you think is going on in the picture?
2. Where does this scene take place?
3. What are the jobs of the three people?
4. Do you think that this picture is funny? Why or why not?

B. Choose one of the three people in the picture and write a paragraph about his/her typical workday. Give the person a name. Follow these steps.

   1. Write four sentences about the person's day.

   _____

   _____

   _____

   _____

   2. Put your sentences in the correct time order. Write a *1* in front of the sentence you think should be first, and so on.

   3. Write your sentences in paragraph form.

   _____

   _____

   _____

   _____

Getting Ready to Write about Special Days

Not all days are typical. Some days are special. In small groups, discuss the following questions about special days and holidays.

   1. How do you celebrate birthdays in your family?
   2. What are the most important holidays in your country?
   3. What are some special traditions associated with holidays?

Try playing Just for Fun: Matching Holidays on page 92.

Writing about Special Days

A. Answer the following questions in complete sentences.

   1. What is your favorite special day or holiday?

   _____

   2. When do you celebrate it?

   _____

   3. How do you celebrate it?

   _____

4. Who do you celebrate this day with?

_____

5. What special foods do you eat on this day?

_____

6. Do you wear special clothes? Do you give or receive gifts?

_____

B. Write a paragraph about your favorite holiday. Use your sentences as a guide. Add any other information that will make your paragraph more interesting. Then, exchange your paragraph with a partner.

_____

_____

_____

_____

_____

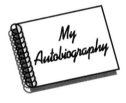

C. Ask your teacher to check your paragraph. Then, copy it over and paste it in your autobiography (p. 101) under the title "My Favorite Holiday."

Writing a Note

Writing notes is a common way to communicate with someone. When you leave a note for someone, it is important to write neatly and give specific information.

A. Read the sample notes below.

Dear Janet,
    Please meet me at the library at 3:30 p.m. I'll be waiting at the main entrance.
            See you later,
            Kathy

Dear Mom,
    I'm meeting Kathy at the library after class. I'll be home around dinner time.
            Janet

B. Write a note for each of the following situations.

1. Write a note to your father. Ask him to pick you up at the mall at 6:00 P.M. Tell him that you will be waiting at the pizza shop on the first floor.

2. Leave a note for your friend Paul. Tell him that you are sorry, but you will not be able to meet him for dinner. Ask him to call you later.

1.

2.

3. Write a note to your roommate, Leslie. Tell her that you had to leave for work early. Also, ask her to return your books to the library.

4. Write a note to your mother. Tell her that her friend Sandy called to wish her a happy birthday. Sandy wants your mother to call her back after dinner.

3.

4.

Writing about Your Hobbies

A. Make a list of three of your favorite hobbies.

1. _____

2. _____

3. _____

B. Add a detail about each hobby on your list.

EXAMPLE:

1. _reading_____ - _I especially like mysteries._____

2. _cooking_____ - _Chinese cooking is my specialty._____

3. _photography_____ - _I usually take black-and-white photos._

1. _____ - _____

2. _____ - _____

3. _____ - _____

C. Use your list as a guide to write a paragraph describing your favorite hobbies. Read the sample paragraph first.

> I have several hobbies. Reading is something I do when I need to relax. I love to read murder mysteries. Another one of my hobbies is cooking. Chinese cooking is my specialty. My favorite hobby is photography. I like to take my pictures in black and white. I think it makes them more interesting. I wish I had more time for each of my hobbies.

Write your paragraph on a separate piece of paper.
After your teacher has checked your paragraph, copy it over, and paste it in your autobiography (p. 101) under the title "My Favorite Hobbies."

On Your Own

A. Choose one of the fictional characters below. Use your imagination to write a paragraph describing a typical day in his/her life. Answer the following questions to help you get started.

a. Snoopy   c. Superman   e. Cinderella
b. Wonder Woman   d. Prince Charming   f. your choice

1. What time do you think the character wakes up and goes to sleep?
2. What does he/she eat for breakfast?
3. What does he/she do in the mornings?
4. What does he/she do in the evenings?

B. Exchange paragraphs with a partner. Read your partner's paragraph and check *yes* or *no* to each question on the Peer Review Checklist. Then help your partner improve his/her paragraph.

Peer Review Checklist

	YES	NO
1. Is the first word of the paragraph indented?	☐	☐
2. Does each sentence begin with a capital letter?	☐	☐
3. Does each sentence end with a period?	☐	☐
4. Does each new sentence begin next to the one before it?	☐	☐
5. Are there any signal words to help guide the reader?	☐	☐
How many? _____		

C. Share your paragraph with your classmates.

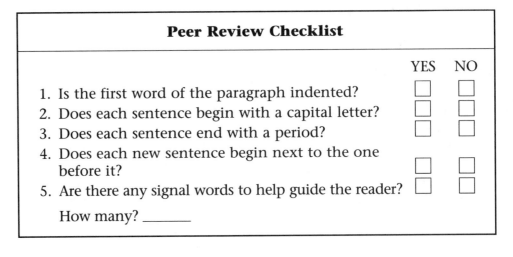

You Be the Editor

A. Read this paragraph. It contains seven mistakes. With a partner, find the seven mistakes and correct them.

> Gary Lesneski is an obstetrician. His work days is never typical. He never know what time a baby will decide to be born. Sometimes he has to go to the hospital in the middle of the night. Other time he stays at home but get many phones calls during the night. Occasionally he sleeps through a entire night without any interruptions. Dr. Lesneski likes him work. No two days are ever the same.

B. Copy your corrected paragraph on the lines below. Then check your work in the Answer Key on page 93.

_____

_____

_____

_____

_____

_____

Writing about Lifestyles

Getting Ready to Write about Physical Fitness

Look at the nine pictures of people exercising below. Label them using the words in the word bank.

Word Bank		
aerobic dancing	rowing	walking
bicycling	running	weight lifting
cross-country skiing	swimming	yoga

Page 1

1. _____

2. _____

3. _____

4. _____

5. _____

6. _____

7. _____

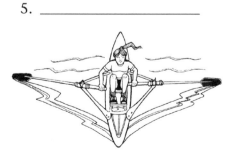

8. _____

9. _____

Answering a Questionnaire about Your Physical Fitness

Answer each of the following questions in complete sentences. Then discuss your answers in small groups.

1. What kind of exercise do you enjoy?

   _____

2. How often do you exercise?

   _____

3. Do you try to eat healthy meals? Why or why not?

   _____

4. Do you smoke? If so, how much and when do you smoke?

   _____

5. Do you usually get enough sleep at night? How many hours of sleep do you like to get?

   _____

6. How do you usually feel after you exercise? energetic? relaxed? tired? hungry?

   _____

Exercise Quiz

Answer the questions on the quiz and then check your answers on page 94 in the Answer Key. Use the word bank on page 29 to help you.

Test Your Exercise IQ

A. What are the five best exercises for your heart and lungs?

   1. _____
   2. _____
   3. _____
   4. _____
   5. _____

B. What five exercises are easiest on your body?

   1. _____
   2. _____
   3. _____
   4. _____
   5. _____

Source: "Dynamic Duo" by David Sharp, *Health*, July/August 1995, pp. 71–74.

Keeping Fit

Many people care about keeping fit and being healthy.

Study the vocabulary in the word bank, read the paragraph that follows and answer the question.

Word Bank		
exercise	keep fit	stay in shape
gym	stay healthy	work out
health club		

Page 1

Steve Fredericks cares about keeping fit. First of all, he tries to get some exercise every day. He belongs to a health club where he usually exercises after work. In addition, he is also careful about his diet. For example, he rarely eats foods that have a lot of fat or sugar. Finally, Steve never smokes cigarettes. Like many of his friends, Steve tries to keep in shape and stay healthy.

What are three things that Steve does to stay healthy?

1. _____

   _____

2. _____

   _____

3. _____

   _____

Frequency Adverbs

When you write or talk about the things that you do, you will often use frequency adverbs. The most common frequency adverbs are *always, usually, often, sometimes, rarely, seldom,* and *never.* These words tell how often something happens or how often you do something.

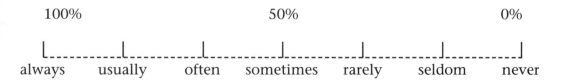

100%   50%   0%

always   usually   often   sometimes   rarely   seldom   never

Adverbs	Examples
always (100% of the time)	I don't have a car. I *always* take the bus to work.
usually	I *usually* get up at 7:00 A.M.
often	We *often* go for a walk after dinner.
sometimes (50% of the time)	I *sometimes* drink coffee after dinner.
rarely	Meryl is on a diet. She *rarely* eats dessert.
seldom	Jeff *seldom* goes to bed before midnight.
never (0% of the time)	Suzanne is a vegetarian. She *never* eats meat.

Using Frequency Adverbs

Complete the following sentences with a frequency adverb that makes the sentence true for you.

1. I _____ exercise in the morning.

2. I _____ smoke cigarettes.

3. I _____ exercise at home.

4. I _____ work out in a gym.

5. I _____ prepare healthy meals.

6. I am _____ in the mood to exercise.

7. I _____ get enough sleep at night.

8. I _____ play organized sports.

9. I _____ feel relaxed after I exercise.

10. I _____ wear sneakers when I work out.

11. I am _____ too tired to jog.

12. I _____ eat at fast-food restaurants.

13. I _____ take vitamins.

Listing Ways to Keep Healthy

With a partner make a list of ways to keep healthy. Think of at least ten ways and write them in complete sentences.

Ways to Keep Healthy
1. *Do not smoke cigarettes.*
2. _____
3. _____
4. _____
5. _____
6. _____
7. _____
8. _____
9. _____
10. _____

Write about What You Do to Stay Healthy

Use the list to write your own paragraph about the things you usually do to stay healthy. Be sure to include some frequency adverbs. Write your paragraph on the lines below.

_____

_____

_____

_____

_____

_____

_____

_____

_____

Paragraph Pointers: Parts of a Paragraph

Most paragraphs have three main parts:
- the topic sentence
- the supporting sentences
- the concluding sentence

A. The first part is called the ***topic sentence.*** This sentence tells the reader what the paragraph is about.

Reread the paragraph about Steve below. Look for the topic sentence.

Steve Fredericks cares about keeping fit. First of all, he tries to get some exercise every day. He belongs to a health club where he usually exercises after work. In addition, he is also careful about his diet. For example, he rarely eats foods that have a lot of fat or sugar. Finally, Steve never smokes cigarettes. Like many of his friends, Steve tries to keep in shape and stay healthy.

Copy the topic sentence here.

_____

B. Next come the ***supporting sentences.*** These sentences use facts, examples, and descriptions to explain the topic sentence. In the paragraph about Steve, there are five supporting sentences.

Copy the five supporting sentences on the lines below.

1. _____
2. _____
3. _____
4. _____
5. _____

C. The last part of a paragraph is called the ***concluding sentence.*** It ties together all of the sentences in the paragraph.

Copy the concluding sentence from the paragraph about Steve here.

_____

A Paragraph Is Like a Sandwich

The topic sentence and concluding sentence are like the two pieces of bread. The supporting sentences are like the lettuce, tomatoes, meat, and cheese that you put between the pieces of bread.

Identifying Parts of a Paragraph

A. Read the following paragraph.

I am usually very lazy on Sundays. I get up late and eat a big breakfast. After breakfast I read the newspaper for a few hours. By four o'clock, I am usually hungry so I make a snack. Then I watch TV and often take a nap. In the evening, I like to go out to dinner with my friends. I am usually back in bed again by ten o'clock. I like to relax on Sunday so that I am ready to start my week on Monday.

Copy the topic sentence of the paragraph here.

_____

Copy the six supporting sentences here.

1. _____

2. _____

3. _____

4. _____

5. _____

6. _____

Copy the concluding sentence here.

_____

B. Now read the next paragraph.

I love to look at my grandparents' old photograph album. It is always fun to see pictures of my mother when she was a little girl. I also enjoy looking at all of the different cars my grandfather bought over the years. It is amazing how much cars have changed. My favorite pictures are the ones of my parents' wedding. I am so glad my grandparents made this album.

Copy the topic sentence of the paragraph here.

_____

Copy the four supporting sentences here.

1. _____
2. _____
3. _____
4. _____

Copy the concluding sentence here.

_____

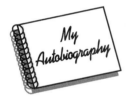

C. Go back to the paragraph you wrote on page 33. Make sure that it has a topic sentence, several supporting sentences, and a concluding sentence. After your teacher has checked your paragraph, copy it over, and paste it in your autobiography (p. 102) under the title "What I Do to Stay Healthy."

Writing Statements from Graphs

A large computer software company in California offered its employees weekly fitness classes. The following graph gives the reasons that thirty of the male employees and forty-nine of the female employees stopped attending the company's fitness classes.

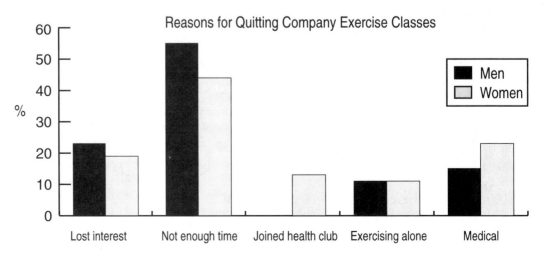

Complete the following sentences.

1. _____ of the men lost interest in the
   fitness classes.

2. The most common reason that both men and women quit the
   classes was _____.

3. A higher percentage of _____ than
   _____ quit the classes and joined a health club.

4. Ten percent of both men and women quit the fitness classes
   because _____.

5. Approximately 12 percent of the men and 15 percent of the
   women quit _____.

On Your Own

A. **Look at the following information about the amount of
   money the average North American and European
   spends every year on vitamin pills.**

United States	$13.30
Germany	$ 9.80
France	$ 7.40
Britain	$ 6.01
Italy	$ 1.01
Spain	$ .48

Source: *Health*, September 1995, p. 44

**Based on the information, write three sentences about
the average amount of money people spend on vitamins
in North America and Europe.**

1. _____

2. _____

3. _____

B. Now answer these questions about the use of vitamins in your country.

1. Do you take vitamins regularly?

   _____

2. Do you think most people in your country take vitamins regularly? Why or why not?

   _____

3. How much do you think the average person in your country spends per year on vitamins?

   _____

C. Use your sentences to write a paragraph about the use of vitamins. Remember to begin with a topic sentence and finish with a concluding sentence.

_____

_____

_____

_____

_____

_____

D. Exchange paragraphs with a partner. Read your partner's paragraph and check *yes* or *no* to each question on the Peer Review Checklist. Then help your partner improve his/her paragraph.

Peer Review Checklist	YES	NO
1. Is the first word of the paragraph indented?	☐	☐
2. Does each sentence begin with a capital letter?	☐	☐
3. Does each sentence end with a period?	☐	☐
4. Does each new sentence begin next to the one before it?	☐	☐
5. Does the paragraph begin with a topic sentence? Underline it.	☐	☐
6. Are there at least three supporting sentences?	☐	☐
7. Is there a concluding sentence? Underline it.	☐	☐

You Be the Editor

A. Read this paragraph. It contains seven mistakes. With a partner, find the seven mistakes and correct them.

There are many benefit of exercise. First of all, regular exercise help people deal with stress. Physical activity also increases your level of energy. People who exercises regularly feel less tired than people who does not. A third benefit are that exercise can help prevent memory loss. If you are active when you are young and stay active, You can help prevent some of the problems of aging. For good mental and physical health, experts recommend twenty to thirty minutes of exercise at least three time per week.

B. Copy your corrected paragraph on the lines below. Then check your work in the Answer Key on page 94.

_____

_____

_____

_____

_____

_____

_____

_____

_____

_____

Writing about People

Getting Ready to Write about People's Appearance

A. Look at the four pictures below. Match the description to the correct picture.

1. _____   2. _____   3. _____   4. _____

a. Mr. Wilcox is tall and thin. He is bald but has a mustache. He wears glasses.

b. Sally has shoulder-length straight blond hair. She has bangs that touch the top of her glasses. She is average height and slender.

c. Dennis has short curly hair. He has a round face with freckles. He is short and plump.

d. Miss Ashley is average height and weight. Her hair is wavy and very long. She has big beautiful eyes, and she wears long earrings.

B. Study the words in the word bank.

Word Bank					
average height	black	curly	mole	short	straight
average weight	blond	fat	mustache	shoulder-length	tall
bald	blue	freckles	plump	skinny	thin
bangs	brown	frizzy	red	slender	wavy
beard	chubby	hazel			

Page 1

C. Use the words from the word bank to complete the chart below.

Hair	Eyes	Height	Weight	Face
wavy		tall		

D. Write a short description of the following people.
Use the words in the word bank to help you.

1. _____

_____

_____

2. _____

_____

_____

Describing What You Look Like

A. Read what a student wrote to describe her appearance.

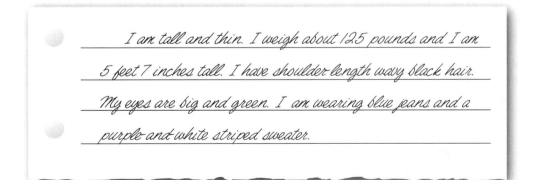

I am tall and thin. I weigh about 125 pounds and I am 5 feet 7 inches tall. I have shoulder-length wavy black hair. My eyes are big and green. I am wearing blue jeans and a purple-and-white striped sweater.

B. Describe what you look like on a separate piece of paper.
Do not put your name on the paper. Fold your paper in half and give it to your teacher. Your teacher will give your paper to another student who will try to guess who wrote the description.

C. When your partner returns your description to you, copy it over, and paste it in your autobiography (p. 102) under the title "What I Look Like."

 Paragraph Pointers: Using Examples

One way to develop a paragraph is to use examples to support your topic sentence.

Fill in the following sentences with examples.

1. There are many places I want to visit. *For example,* I would

   love to see _____, _____,

   and _____.

2. Several of my friends are good athletes. *For instance,*

   _____, _____, and

   _____ are all good at sports.

3. Many inventions have made our lives easier. *For example,*

   _____, _____, and

   _____ have all made our day-to-day

   activities easier.

Writing a Paragraph with Examples

A. Here is a paragraph that uses examples.

I am a very organized person. For example, I organize my clothes according to the season when I wear them. I organize my sweaters and shoes by color. I organize our books by their topics. I also like to keep the cooking spices in alphabetical order so that they are always easy to find. My husband makes fun of me and says that I am too organized. However, I never lose anything, and he is always looking for something.

B. Rewrite the paragraph changing the word *I* in the first sentence to *Rachel*. Be sure to make all of the necessary grammatical changes.

_____

_____

_____

_____

_____

_____

_____

_____

Describing People's Character

A. Choose one person you know well. The person can be a friend, relative, neighbor, classmate, teacher, or anyone else you know very well. Write his/her name on the line.

_____

B. Write one adjective from the word bank that describes the person you chose.

_____

Word Bank					
ambitious	dependable	hardworking	messy	quiet	shy
artistic	energetic	helpful	neat	responsible	social
boring	enthusiastic	honest	optimistic	selfish	studious
brave	friendly	jealous	organized	sensitive	talkative
competitive	funny	kind	patient	serious	thrifty
creative	generous	lazy			

Page 1

C. Write the topic sentence for a paragraph about the person. Include both the name of the person and the adjective you chose.

EXAMPLE: *My sister Suzanne is the most dependable person in my family.*

_____

D. Make a list of at least three examples that support your topic sentence.

EXAMPLES:

1. _I can always depend on her to give me a ride to work._
2. _She is never late._
3. _She is the one everyone in the family turns to when we have a problem and need good advice._

1. _____

2. _____

3. _____

E. Use your list as a guide to write a paragraph.

_____

_____

_____

_____

Describing Your Own Character

On a separate piece of paper, write a paragraph about your character, using the word bank on page 43 and giving examples. After your teacher has checked your paragraph, copy it over, and paste it in your autobiography (p. 103) under the title "The Way I Am."

Use Your Imagination

A. Look back at the picture "The Window Washer" on page 22. How would you describe each of the three people? What words would you use to describe each one's character?

1. The secretary: _____

2. The boss: _____

3. The window washer: _____

B. Use your imagination to write about one of the people in the picture.

_____

_____

_____

Writing from a Time Line

A. Look at the following time line that contains information about Amelia Earhart.
Amelia Earhart is one of North America's greatest heroines. She was a famous aviator who opened the door for other female pilots.

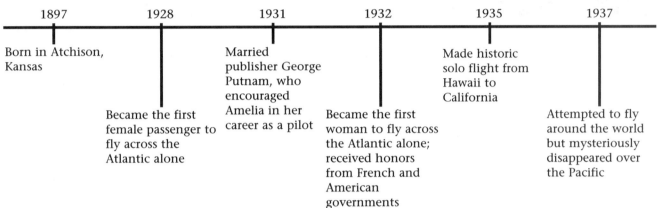

| 1897 | 1928 | 1931 | 1932 | 1935 | 1937 |

Born in Atchison, Kansas

Became the first female passenger to fly across the Atlantic alone

Married publisher George Putnam, who encouraged Amelia in her career as a pilot

Became the first woman to fly across the Atlantic alone; received honors from French and American governments

Made historic solo flight from Hawaii to California

Attempted to fly around the world but mysteriously disappeared over the Pacific

1. Write at least one complete sentence for each fact on the time line.

   Amelia Earhart was born in 1897 in Atchison, Kansas.

   _____

   _____

   _____

   _____

   _____

2. Use your sentences to write a paragraph about Amelia Earhart.

   The famous aviator Amelia Earhart was born in 1897 in Atchison, Kansas.

   _____

   _____

   _____

   _____

   _____

B. Seiji Ozawa is an important orchestra conductor who is famous all over the world.

1935	1952	1960	1961–1962	1965–1970	1973–
Born of Japanese parents in Hoten, China		Won Koussevitzky Award for excellence in conducting		Served as conductor of the Toronto Symphony	
	Injured in a rugby accident, turned from piano playing to conducting		Was assistant to Leonard Bernstein, conductor of the New York Philharmonic Orchestra		Became music director of the Boston Symphony Orchestra

1. Write at least one sentence for each fact on the time line.

_____

_____

_____

_____

_____

_____

2. Use your sentences to write a paragraph about Seiji Ozawa.

_____

_____

_____

_____

_____

_____

_____

C. Michael Jordan is a professional basketball player.

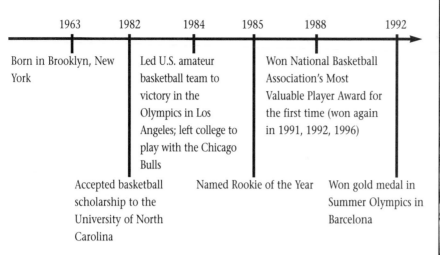

| 1963 | 1982 | 1984 | 1985 | 1988 | 1992 |

Born in Brooklyn, New York

Led U.S. amateur basketball team to victory in the Olympics in Los Angeles; left college to play with the Chicago Bulls

Won National Basketball Association's Most Valuable Player Award for the first time (won again in 1991, 1992, 1996)

Accepted basketball scholarship to the University of North Carolina

Named Rookie of the Year

Won gold medal in Summer Olympics in Barcelona

1. Write at least one sentence for each fact on the time line.

_____

_____

_____

_____

_____

_____

2. Use your sentences to write a paragraph about Michael Jordan.

_____

_____

_____

_____

_____

_____

_____

_____

D. Make a time line of the important events in your own life.

1. Write at least one sentence for each fact on your time line.

_____

_____

_____

_____

_____

_____

2. Use your sentences to write a paragraph about yourself.

_____

_____

_____

_____

_____

_____

_____

_____

Writing about Well-Known People

A. Use the information in the fact sheet about Gabriel García Márquez to write a short paragraph about him.

Name:	Gabriel García Márquez
Place of birth:	Aracataca, Colombia
Year of birth:	1928
Occupation:	Author
Best-known novel:	*One Hundred Years of Solitude*
Prize:	Nobel Prize in literature, 1982

_____

_____

_____

_____

_____

B. Now do the same with the following information about Martina Navratilova.

Name:	Martina Navratilova
Place of birth:	Prague, Czechoslovakia
Year of birth:	1956
Occupation:	Professional tennis player
Accomplishments:	National champion in her native country from 1972–1975, top-ranked women's tennis player for many years, broke the record of titles won in 1992

_____

_____

_____

_____

_____

On Your Own

A. Choose a famous person you would like to write about.
Write his/her name here.

_____

B. Draw a time line that includes at least four important events about his/her life.

C. Write a sentence for each event that you put on the time line.

_____

_____

_____

_____

_____

_____

D. Exchange papers with a partner. Make sure you understand each other's sentences. Rewrite any sentences that are not clear.

E. Write your paragraph. Include the person's name in your topic sentence.

_____

_____

_____

_____

_____

_____

_____

_____

F. Exchange paragraphs with a partner. Read your partner's paragraph and check *yes* or *no* to each question on the Peer Review Checklist. Then help your partner improve his/her paragraph.

Peer Review Checklist		
	YES	NO
1. Is the first word of the paragraph indented?	☐	☐
2. Does each sentence begin with a capital letter?	☐	☐
3. Does each sentence end with a period?	☐	☐
4. Does each new sentence begin next to the one before it?	☐	☐
5. Does the paragraph begin with a topic sentence? Underline it.	☐	☐
6. Are there examples to support the topic sentence? How many? _____	☐	☐

You Be the Editor

A. Read the following paragraph. It contains seven mistakes. With a partner, find the seven mistakes and correct them.

John Fitzgerald Kennedy was born in May 29, 1917, in Brookline, Massachusetts. She graduated from Harvard University in 1940. From 1941 in 1945, he served in the United States Navy. On 1953, he marries Jacqueline Lee Bouvier in Newport, Rhode Island. He was elected president of the United States in 1960. Kennedy is assassinated three years later in November 22, 1963, in Dallas, Texas.

B. Copy your corrected paragraph on the lines below. Then check your work in the Answer Key on page 94.

_____

_____

_____

_____

_____

_____

_____

_____

_____

_____

Writing about Places

Getting Ready to Write about Places

Read the following letter.

Dear Mom,

I just moved into my new apartment, and it already feels like home. It's in a nice building a few blocks from school. The thing I like most about the apartment is that it's very sunny. There are big windows in every room. It has a large living room with a fireplace along the north wall. The kitchen is small, but the appliances are new. A long hall next to the kitchen leads to the bedroom and bathroom. The only problem is that the closet in the bedroom is very small. I can't wait for you to visit me.

Love,
Elaine

Describing Where You Live

A. Answer these questions about your house or apartment.

1. What do you like most about your home?

   _____

2. What do you like least about your home?

   _____

3. How many rooms does it have? Name the rooms.

   _____

4. How big is each room?

   _____

B. Now describe your home in a letter to a friend or relative on a separate piece of paper. Use the letter on page 53 as a guide. After your teacher has checked your letter, copy it over, and paste it in your autobiography (p. 103) under the title "My Home."

Prepositions of Place

When you want to tell where something is located, you will need to use prepositions. The following prepositions will help you describe where items are located in relation to other items.

over	beside	in front of	on	next to
in back of	in	between	behind	under

Using Prepositions of Place

A. Look at each of the following pictures. Then complete the sentences by using the correct prepositions from the list above.

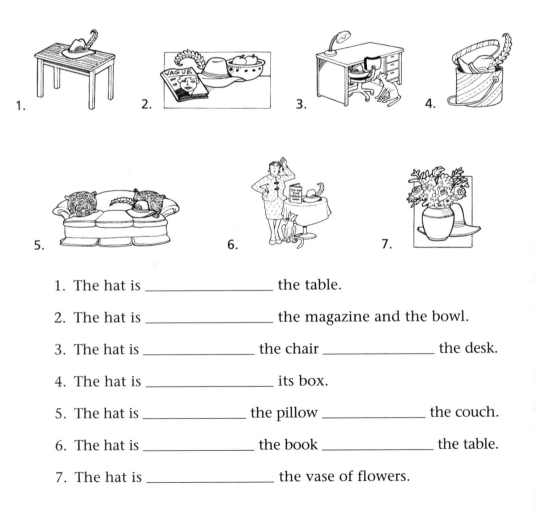

1. The hat is _____ the table.

2. The hat is _____ the magazine and the bowl.

3. The hat is _____ the chair _____ the desk.

4. The hat is _____ its box.

5. The hat is _____ the pillow _____ the couch.

6. The hat is _____ the book _____ the table.

7. The hat is _____ the vase of flowers.

8. The hat is _____ the dog.

9. The hat is _____ the table _____ the couch.

10. The cat is jumping _____ the hat.

8.   9.   10.

B. Look at the following scene. Practice using prepositions of place by adding each of the following items to the scene.

1. Draw a bowl of fruit in front of the grandmother.
2. Draw a dog under the table.
3. Draw a ball beside the dog.
4. Draw a toy next to the ball.
5. Draw a clock on the wall behind the grandfather.
6. Draw a chandelier over the table.
7. Draw a vase between the candles on the table.
8. Draw a flower in the vase.
9. Draw a cake on the long table behind the mother.
10. Draw a painting on the wall over the long table.

Describing a Picture

Write three sentences that describe the photograph. Use prepositions.

1. _____

2. _____

3. _____

Describing a Room

A. Look at the pictures of the three dormitory rooms. In small groups, discuss each picture and make a list of the things in each room. Use the word bank to help you.

Word Bank				
art supplies	clock	fishing gear	phone	tennis racket
bed	closet	hockey stick	poster	TV
bedspread	computer	ice skates	Rollerblades	vase
bookcase	curtains	lamp	rug	VCR
books	desk	nightstand	skis	wastebasket
chair	dresser	painting canvas	stereo	

Page 1

Room 1

_____

_____

_____

_____

_____

Room 2

_____

_____

_____

_____

_____

Room 3

_____

_____

_____

_____

_____

B. What adjectives would you use to describe each room?

Use the word bank to help you. Try to add some other words.

Word Bank		
clean	messy	organized
cluttered	neat	small
cozy	orderly	sunny
large		

Page 1

Room 1	Room 2	Room 3
messy	_____	_____
_____	_____	_____
_____	_____	_____

C. Choose one of the rooms and write a description of the room and the person who lives in it.

_____

_____

_____

_____

_____

_____

_____

_____

_____

_____

Writing a Postcard

A. Read the following postcard that was sent from the Grand Canyon in Arizona. It shows the correct form for writing and addressing a postcard.

Dear Aya,

The Grand Canyon is awesome! Yesterday we took the helicopter tour over the canyon. Tomorrow we are going to ride mules down to the bottom. You must see this before you go back home to Japan. See you soon.

Love,

Muriel

Ms. Aya Ochiai
551 West Cedar Street
Ann Arbor, Michigan 48105

B. Use the space below to draw a simple picture that shows a place you have visited. Then write a message to a friend or relative. Address the postcard correctly.

Writing about Your Hometown

Write a paragraph describing your hometown to your classmates. Follow these steps.

1. Complete the topic sentence below.

   My hometown, _____, is a _____ place.
   (name of town)   (adjective)

2. Make a list of the information you want to include in your paragraph in the supporting sentences.

   _____   _____

   _____   _____

   _____   _____

3. Write a concluding sentence about your hometown.

   _____

4. Use your information to write a paragraph. Write it on a separate piece of paper. After your teacher has checked your paragraph, copy it over, and paste it in your autobiography (p. 104) under the title "My Hometown."

Writing a Letter

The following letter has been started for you. Read the beginning and then finish the letter.

> Dear _____ ,
>
>   I was so happy when you called to tell me that you were planning to come to _____ to visit me. There are many things to do and see here, but I think the most _____ place is
>
> _____ . _____
>
> _____
>
> _____
>
> _____
>
>   Love,
>
>   _____

Addressing an Envelope

A. Look at the sample envelope.

Toby Boxer
52 Walden Street
Ames, Iowa 50010

Ms. Charlotte Brown
234 Benefit Street
Providence, Rhode Island 02912

B. Address the envelope to the person you wrote your letter to on page 59. Put your name and address in the upper left corner. Then put the person's name and address in the middle.

Writing a Haiku

Haiku is a very old form of poetry. It originated in Japan over 700 years ago. It is still an important part of Japanese culture and is also popular in English. Haiku poems are usually about nature.

The form of a haiku is always the same. It contains three lines:

> The first line has five syllables.
> The second line has seven syllables.
> The third line has five syllables.

Here are some examples that students have written.

Look up in the sky
See the blue birds flying high
Over the ocean

Vasakorn Bhadranavik

Noisy rain has stopped
White snow covers everything
Silent night has come

Kazu Karasawa

The birds of passage
Are taking a winter's rest
Ready to go south

Fumihiko Suita

渡り鳥
骨を休めて
行く準備

Writing Your Own Haiku

1. Choose a season and a scene from nature that you would like to write about.

   season: _____

   scene from nature: _____

   _____

2. Think about the picture that you want to create in your readers' minds. Make some notes here. Use the examples on page 61 to help you.

   _____

   _____

   _____

3. Decide what your first line will be. Work on the words until you have exactly five syllables.

   _____

4. Write your second line. Remember that it must contain seven syllables.

   _____

5. Write your third line. Make sure it contains five syllables.

   _____

6. Write your haiku below.

   _____

   _____

   _____

7. Exchange your haiku with a partner. Make sure you understand your partner's haiku. Make sure the syllable count is correct for each line.

8. Rewrite your haiku on a separate sheet of paper. Illustrate your haiku as in the examples and display it in your classroom. When your haiku is returned to you, paste it in your autobiography (p. 104) under the title "My Haiku."

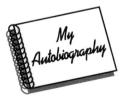

On Your Own

A. Look out a window and think about the view. Write a paragraph describing what you see.

_____

_____

_____

_____

_____

_____

_____

_____

_____

_____

_____

_____

_____

B. Exchange paragraphs with a partner. Read your partner's paragraph and check *yes* or *no* to each question on the Peer Review Checklist. Then help your partner improve his/her paragraph.

Peer Review Checklist	YES	NO
1. Is the first word of the paragraph indented?	☐	☐
2. Does each sentence begin with a capital letter?	☐	☐
3. Does each sentence end with a period?	☐	☐
4. Does each new sentence begin next to the one before it?	☐	☐
5. Does the paragraph begin with a topic sentence? Underline it.	☐	☐
6. Are there examples to support the topic sentence?	☐	☐
How many? _____		

You Be the Editor

A. Read the following paragraph. It contains seven mistakes. With a partner, find the seven mistakes and correct them.

Honolulu is a great place to go for a family vacation because it offer something for everyone. For example, Waikiki Beach is perfect for anyone who enjoys water sports? It is one of the most famous beaches and surfing areas in the world. The hikers in your family will want to climb Diamond Head. Is a 760-foot volcanic crater. The shopping in fabulous is Honolulu. Hawaiian arts and crafts is very popular. Some members of your family might enjoy going to a hula show or a luau dinner in the evening. Other examples of populars activities include the aquarium, the zoo, and the rain forest.

B. Copy your corrected paragraph on the lines below. Then check your work in the Answer Key on page 95.

_____

_____

_____

_____

_____

_____

_____

_____

_____

Writing a Description

Getting Ready to Write a Description

A. Look at the pictures below from The International Gift Shop catalog. Write the name of the item in each picture on the line provided. Use the words in the word bank below to help you.

Word Bank

rug	gloves	pattern	stripes
clay	mirror	plate	tablecloth
cotton	napkin	sheets	towels
design	necklace	silk	wool

Page 1

1. _____

2. _____

3. _____

4. _____

5. _____

B. Read the following description of each item. Then complete the sentences with the correct noun. Use the pictures on page 65 and the words from the word bank.

1. These 100% cotton Turkish _____ have blue and white stripes. They are very large and soft. They are so thick and absorbent that you will want to use them at home and at the beach. You can order a set of three for only $35.

2. This beautiful _____ from Brazil will make a nice gift for someone special. The large oval amethyst hangs from an 18-inch gold chain. You can have this elegant piece of jewelry for $90.

3. These soft leather _____ are made in Italy and will keep your hands warm in winter. They come in sizes small, medium, and large. They are available in brown or black. Buy them for yourself, or give them as a gift for $25.

4. This 15-inch round _____ is from Mexico. It is made of clay. The interesting design includes drawings of flowers, trees, birds, and fish. The natural colors look nice in any room. We are offering you this attractive item for only $20, so order it right away.

5. This rectangular _____ is made of silk and wool. It is 3 feet wide and 6 feet long. It was made by hand in China. The geometric pattern is based on the Chinese symbol for happiness. You can own this beautiful floor covering for a special price of $530.

C. Complete the sentences below, using the adjectives in this word bank.

Word Bank			
absorbent	flowered	rectangular	soft
attractive	geometric	round	thick
beautiful	oval	smooth	thin
elegant			

Page 1

1. The Chinese rug is _____ in shape.

2. The Turkish towels are very _____.

3. The Brazilian necklace has a large _____ amethyst hanging from a gold chain.

4. The Italian gloves are made of _____ leather.

5. The _____ Mexican plate is made of clay.

Filling Out an Order Form

You want to order something from The International Gift Shop catalog on page 65.

Fill out the following form.

THE INTERNATIONAL GIFT SHOP					**Ship To:** Name		
ORDER TOLL FREE					Address		
1-800-371-2311					City		
					State	Zip	

Item Number	Qty.	Item Description	Color	✔ for Gift Wrap	Unit Price	Total Price

Gift Wrap	**Payment Method**	**Merchandise Total**	
Your gift orders receive special care. With any gift order, we will print your message on the packing slip. If you request, for $3.75 per box, we will wrap your gifts in our red gift paper, trimmed with a gold ribbon, and include your message printed on a gift card. Use the gift-order sections provided on the order form.	Enclose your personal check, money order, gift certificate, or credit card information. ❑ Check ❑ Credit Card ❑ Money Order ❑ Certificate (#_____) Card Account Number Month Year ❒❒❒❒❒❒❒❒❒❒❒❒❒❒ ❒❒❒❒ Signature of Authorized Buyer _____	Add $3.75 for each gift wrap checked	
		SUBTOTAL	
		$2.00 Shipping Charge	
		6% Sales Tax	
		TOTAL	

Writing a Thank-You Note

You received one of the five items from The International Gift Shop catalog as a birthday gift from a good friend.

Write a thank-you note to your friend. Include a description of the gift and tell why you liked it.

THANK YOU
_____ (date)
Dear _____,
_____
_____
_____
_____,
_____

Writing a Description for a Gift Shop Catalog

Find a photograph in a magazine or draw a picture of a product your country is known for. Use the picture to write a description for The International Gift Shop catalog. Be sure to include the price.

Getting Ready to Write about Clothes

Look at the pictures below of four fashion models. Match the description to the correct picture.

1. _____ 2. _____ 3. _____ 4. _____

a. Yoshi has on a striped shirt and jeans. He is wearing a leather belt and sneakers.

b. Juanita is wearing a short checked wool skirt with a white blouse and a V-necked sweater. She also has on tights and boots.

c. Sam is wearing a turtleneck with a vest and blazer. He has on gray slacks and loafers.

d. Pamela is wearing a suit and pumps. She is wearing a pearl necklace.

Writing about a Fashion Show

A. Study the words in the word bank.

		Word Bank		
argyle socks	cable knit sweater	necklace	scarf	tie shoes
barrette	checked	plaid	shorts	tights
belt and buckle	earrings	pleated skirt	slacks	turtleneck
blazer	gloves	polka dots	sneakers	vest
blouse	jeans	polo shirt	striped	V-necked sweater
button-down collar	loafers	pumps	suit	

Page 1

B. Work with a partner to complete the following steps.

1. Make a list of the clothes that your partner is wearing. Use the words from the word bank to help you. Be sure to ask your teacher if you need help with the name of a pattern, a color, or a piece of jewelry that is not included in the word bank.

_____

_____

_____

_____

_____

2. Present your partner as a fashion model. Use the lines below to write down what you want to say about what your partner is wearing. Remember to start with your partner's name.

_____

_____

_____

_____

_____

_____

Getting Ready to Write about Cars

Look at the pictures of the inside and the outside of a car.
Label the parts of the car using words from the word bank.

Word Bank

accelerator	clutch	heat and air controls	rearview mirror	taillight
airbag	dashboard	hood	roof	tape deck
ashtray	directional signal	hubcap	seatbelt	tire
brake	emergency brake	ignition	side mirror	trunk
bucket seat	gas tank	license plate	steering wheel	windshield
bumper	gearshift	radio	stickshift	windshield wiper
CD player	headlight			

Page 1

Writing about Your Dream Car

1. Find a photograph of your dream car in a magazine or draw your own dream car.
2. Describe your picture to a partner.
3. Write at least three sentences that describe your dream car.

   EXAMPLE: _My dream car is red._

   a. _____

   b. _____

   c. _____

4. Write a general sentence that you can use as a topic sentence for your paragraph.

   _____

5. Write about your dream car in paragraph form.

   _____

   _____

   _____

   _____

6. Exchange paragraphs with your partner. Make sure that you understand your partner's paragraph completely. Suggest changes that you think are necessary.
7. Rewrite your paragraph on a separate piece of paper and paste it, along with your picture of your dream car, in your autobiography (p. 105) under the title "My Dream Car."

On Your Own

A. Draw a picture of the uniform of your favorite sports team.

B. Write a short paragraph describing the uniform.

C. Exchange paragraphs with a partner. Read your partner's paragraph and check *yes* or *no* to each question on the Peer Review Checklist. Then help your partner improve his/her paragraph.

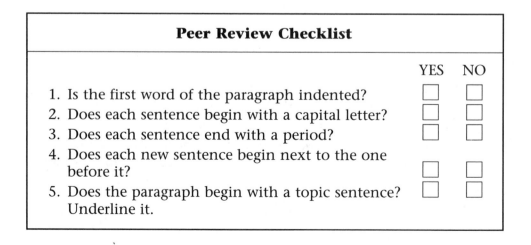

Peer Review Checklist		
	YES	NO
1. Is the first word of the paragraph indented?	☐	☐
2. Does each sentence begin with a capital letter?	☐	☐
3. Does each sentence end with a period?	☐	☐
4. Does each new sentence begin next to the one before it?	☐	☐
5. Does the paragraph begin with a topic sentence? Underline it.	☐	☐

You Be the Editor

A. Read the following paragraph. It contains seven mistakes. With a partner, find the seven mistakes and correct them.

     The Loch Ness monster is large animal that many people believe lives in a lake in northern Scotland. Hundreds of people say that they have seen the animal. In their descriptions, they say that it is about 30 foot (9.14 meters) long and 6 feet (1.85 meters) wide. It looks like a dinosaur. They say that it has two fin like a fish, two hump like a camel, and long, thin neck. The earliest descriptions of the loch ness monster go back to the year A.D. 565.

B. Copy your corrected paragraph on the lines below. Then check your work in the Answer Key on page 95.

_____

_____

_____

_____

_____

_____

_____

_____

_____

_____

Writing Instructions

Getting Ready to Write a Recipe

A. Look at the six pictures below. They show the steps involved in making a yogurt milkshake. Find the sentence from the list below that goes with each picture. Match the sentence to the correct picture.

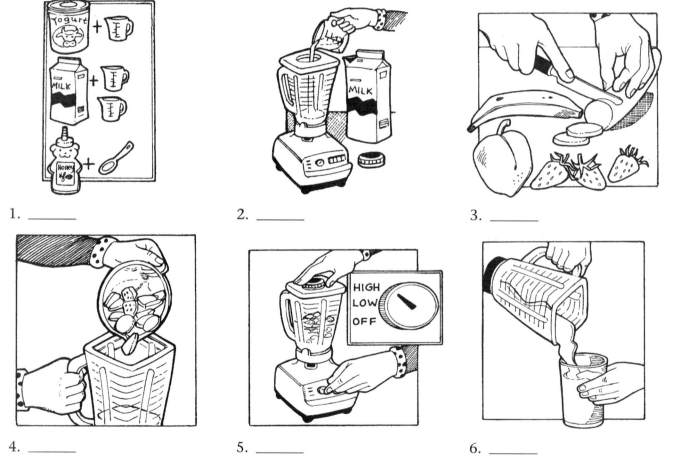

1. _____

2. _____

3. _____

4. _____

5. _____

6. _____

a. Then cut up some fresh fruit. You can use a banana, a peach, and some strawberries.

b. First you need one cup of yogurt, two cups of milk, and one tablespoon of honey.

c. Add the fruit to the milk and yogurt.

d. Pour the yogurt, milk, and honey into a blender.

e. Pour the milkshake into a tall glass and enjoy your nutritious snack.

f. Put the top on the blender and blend on high for one minute.

B. Use the sentences from the previous activity to complete a paragraph about how to make a yogurt milkshake.

When you want a delicious and healthy snack, try this yogurt milkshake.

_____

_____

_____

_____

_____

Writing a Recipe

Prepare one of your favorite dishes. Bring it to class to share with your classmates. Fill out the recipe card below. First make a list of the ingredients. Then write the instructions for how to prepare the dish. Use the words in the word bank below to help you.

Word Bank					
bake	chop	cut	grill	mix	sauté
boil	combine	fry	heat	peel	simmer
broil	cook	garnish	melt	pour	stir

Page 1

_____
(name of dish)

Ingredients: _____

_____

_____

_____

_____

Instructions: _____

_____

_____

_____

_____

Getting Ready to Write Helpful Hints

A. Look at the five pictures. They show how to remove an ink stain from a piece of clothing. Then read the list of steps that follows. Put the steps in the correct order.

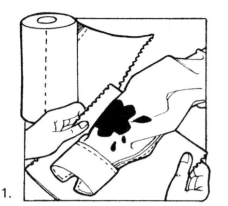

1.

2.

3.

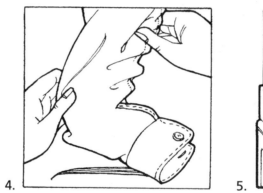

4.

5.

_____ Then spray the stain with aerosol hair spray.

_____ After that, rub the stain gently with a clean cloth.

_____ First, put a paper towel under the stain.

_____ Finally, wash the piece of clothing as usual.

_____ Continue rubbing until the stain is completely gone.

B. Use the steps to complete the paragraph that follows.

This is what you need to do in order to remove an ink stain from clothing.

_____

_____

_____

_____

_____

Writing Helpful Hints

A. Look at the six pictures. They show how to clean silver jewelry. Write a sentence for each picture.

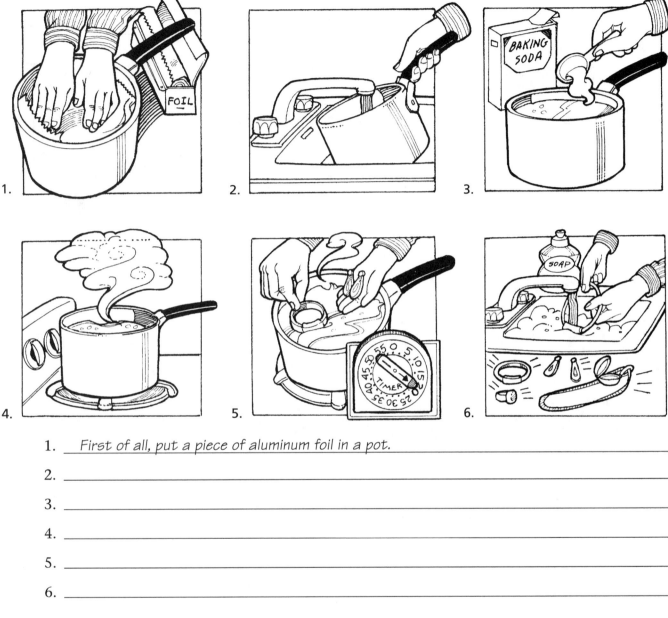

1. ___First of all, put a piece of aluminum foil in a pot.___

2. _____

3. _____

4. _____

5. _____

6. _____

B. Now put your sentences in paragraph form. The topic sentence is given.

___Here is an easy way to clean silver jewelry.___

_____

_____

_____

_____

Getting Ready to Write First-Aid Instructions

A. Look at the five pictures. They show what to do if you get a nosebleed. Then read the list of steps that follow. Put the steps in the correct order.

1.

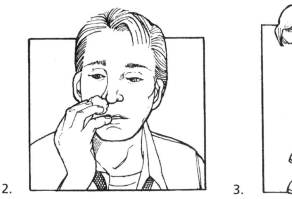

2.

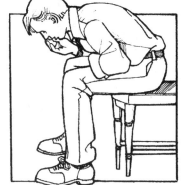

3.

4.

5.

_____ Put a cotton pad in the bleeding nostril.

_____ Squeeze your nose until it stops bleeding.

_____ If your nose continues to bleed, call a doctor.

_____ Then sit down with your head leaning forward.

_____ First, loosen the clothing around your neck.

B. Use the steps to complete the paragraph that follows.

You should follow these steps if you get a nosebleed.

_____

_____

_____

_____

_____

Writing First-Aid Instructions

A. Look at the six pictures. They show the procedure for taking care of frostbitten toes. Write a sentence for each picture.

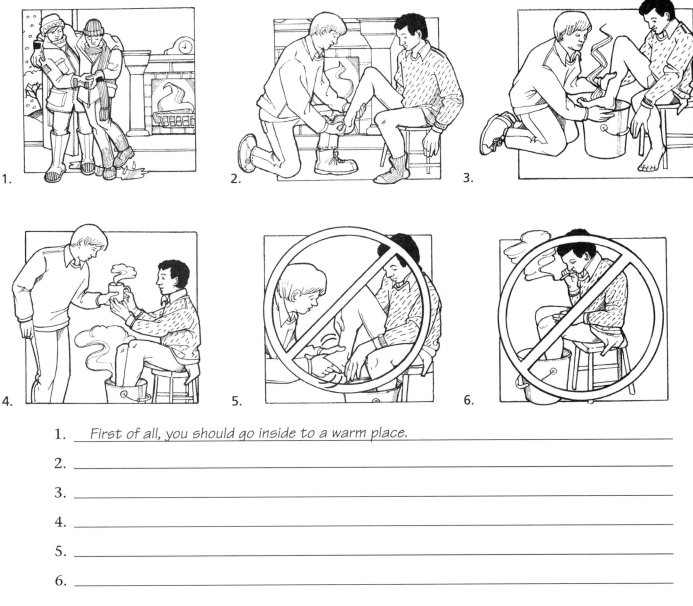

1. ___First of all, you should go inside to a warm place.___ _____

2. _____

3. _____

4. _____

5. _____

6. _____

B. Now put your sentences in paragraph form. The topic sentence is given.

___If you are out in the cold and your toes become frostbitten, follow this first-aid procedure.___

_____

_____

_____

_____

```
┌─────────────────────────────────────────────────────┐
│  ☞          Paragraph Pointers:                       │
│        Putting Ideas in Time Order                    │
├─────────────────────────────────────────────────────┤
│  When you want to tell someone how to do something,   │
│  the first thing you need to do is make a list of the │
│  steps in the process. Then you should arrange the    │
│  steps according to time order. When you write your   │
│  paragraph, you should use signal words to help       │
│  guide your reader from one step to the next. You can │
│  use the same signal words you used when you wrote    │
│  about your daily activities (Chapter 3).             │
│                                                       │
│            TIME-ORDER SIGNAL WORDS                    │
│                                                       │
│               first, second, third                   │
│               first of all                           │
│               then                                    │
│               after that                              │
│               next                                    │
│               finally                                 │
│                                                       │
└─────────────────────────────────────────────────────┘
```

Using Time-Order Signal Words

Complete the following paragraphs using time-order signal words.

1. It is easy to get a good picture of your cat if you follow these steps. _____ give your cat something to eat. When she is full, move your cat to a sunny window. _____ rub your cat's back for a few minutes until she falls asleep. As soon as she wakes up, get in position and have your camera ready. _____ take the picture as she yawns and stretches.

2. In order to get a driver's license in the United States you need to follow these steps. _____ you need to fill out an application at the Department of Motor Vehicles in the state where you live. _____ you have to take and pass a written test on the traffic signs and driving laws. You also have to pass a vision test. _____ you must take a road test with an examiner who will make sure that you can drive safely. Once you pass the road test, you will get your driver's license.

Writing about How to Do Something

A. Choose one of the following processes to write about:

- How to give your pet a bath
- How to pack for a weekend at the beach
- How to build a campfire
- How to fall asleep
- How to fix a broken heart
- How to cure the hiccups
- How to cure a cold

B. Make a list of all the steps in the process. Then put the steps in the correct time order.

_____

_____

_____

_____

_____

_____

_____

C. Write a paragraph describing the process. Use the list of steps as a guide. Remember to begin with a clear topic sentence that states the process you are describing. Also be sure to include some signal words to help guide your reader.

_____

_____

_____

_____

_____

_____

_____

_____

_____

_____

Taking Telephone Messages

A. Read the following telephone conversation. Then leave a message for Dana.

```
TELEPHONE MESSAGE

TO: _____

_____

_____

_____

_____
```

YOU: Hello.

CALLER: Hi, Sandy. This is Joel. Is Dana there?

YOU: No. She just left. She'll be back in a few minutes.

CALLER: Please tell her that I have to work late tonight, so I will pick her up at 9:30.

YOU: OK. I'll make sure she gets the message.

CALLER: Thanks, Sandy. Bye.

B. You are at the office and the phone rings. You answer. Leave a message for Joan.

```
TELEPHONE MESSAGE

TO: _____

_____

_____

_____

_____
```

YOU: Good morning. Seasons Software Corporation.

CALLER: Hello. Is Joan there?

YOU: No. I'm sorry, she's out of the office this morning. Can I take a message?

CALLER: Yes. This is Sylvia Barrows calling. Please tell her that I called about our meeting tomorrow. Would you ask her to call me back?

YOU: Certainly. Does she have your number?

CALLER: I'm not sure. Let me give it to you. It is 215-884-2714.

YOU: I'll make sure she gets the message.

CALLER: Thank you. Bye.

YOU: Bye.

On Your Own

A. Choose one of the following topics and write a process paragraph on a separate piece of paper.

- How to clean something (your room, your car, etc.)
- How to fix something (a flat tire, a broken vase, etc.)
- How to cook or bake something
- How to play something (checkers, soccer, etc.)
- One of the other paragraph topics from the list on page 81

B. Exchange paragraphs with a partner. Read your partner's paragraph and check *yes* or *no* to each question on the Peer Review Checklist. Then help your partner improve his/her paragraph.

Peer Review Checklist		
	YES	NO
1. Is the first word of the paragraph indented?	☐	☐
2. Does each sentence begin with a capital letter?	☐	☐
3. Does each sentence end with a period?	☐	☐
4. Does each new sentence begin next to the one before it?	☐	☐
5. Does the paragraph begin with a topic sentence?	☐	☐
6. Are the sentences in correct time order?	☐	☐
7. Are there signal words to help guide the reader? Circle them.	☐	☐

You Be the Editor

A. Read the following paragraph. It contains seven mistakes. With a partner, find the seven mistakes and correct them.

Driving on a wet or slippery road can be danger. If your car start to skid, this tips may be helpful. Firstofall, slowly take your foot off the gas pedal. Turns the steering wheel slowly and only as much as necessary to keep your car on the road. Next, if you have to use your brakes, pumps them gently up and down. Final, do not try to stop or turn quickly.

B. Copy your corrected paragraph on the lines below. Then check your work in the Answer Key on page 95.

_____

_____

_____

_____

_____

_____

Writing about Past Events

Getting Ready to Write: Organizing by Time

A. Look at the four pictures. They tell a story, but they are not in the correct order. Number the pictures so they tell the story in a logical time order.

B. Write one sentence that tells what is happening in each picture. Make sure your sentences are in the correct time order.

Picture 1: _____

Picture 2: _____

Picture 3: _____

Picture 4: _____

C. Write the story in paragraph form.

_____

_____

_____

_____

_____

_____

☞ **Paragraph Pointers: Narrative Paragraphs**

A narrative paragraph tells a story. When you write a story, it is very important to write the sequence of events in the right time order:

- The topic sentence should tell the time and place of the story.
- The rest of the sentences should tell what happened in the correct time order.

Practicing Time Order

A. Read the following paragraph about a trip to Chicago. The story does not make sense because the sentences are not in the right order.

> My friend called an ambulance and it took me to the hospital. On the first day I was there, I fell down on an icy sidewalk and broke my wrist. Last week I went to Chicago to visit a friend. I spent my vacation in Chicago General Hospital.

B. Rewrite the story so that the sentences are in the right order.

_____

_____

_____

_____

Writing a Narrative Paragraph

A. Discuss this picture in small groups.

   1. Discuss where the scene takes place.
   2. Decide what is happening in the picture.
   3. Talk about when the event is happening.
   4. Describe the people in the picture.

B. Based on the picture and your group discussion, write your own story that tells what is happening.

_____

_____

_____

_____

_____

Finishing a Story

A. Complete the following narrative paragraphs. The topic sentences are given.

1. _One of the funniest memories I have of my childhood happened when I was_ _____ _years old._

_____

_____

_____

_____

_____

2. _A very _____ thing happened to me on my first _____

_____

_____

_____

_____

_____

3. _One summer my friends and I had a(n) _____ experience. _____

_____

_____

_____

_____

_____

4. _My trip to _____ was very _____

_____

_____

_____

_____

_____

_____

5. _One of the most enjoyable evenings I have ever spent was the time I _____

_____

_____

_____

_____

_____

B. Choose one of your paragraphs and exchange it with a partner. Make sure you understand your partner's paragraph completely. Suggest changes that you think are necessary.

C. Copy your corrected paragraph on a separate piece of paper. Paste it in your autobiography (p. 106) under the title "My Finished Story."

Writing about Memories

A. Think of a memorable experience from your past that you would like to share with your classmates. It should be a time when you were scared, embarrassed, happy, or sad.

B. Tell the story orally to your classmates in three minutes. Be sure to include who, when, where, and what.

C. Write about your memorable experience in paragraph form.

_____

_____

_____

_____

_____

_____

_____

_____

Using Poetry to Write about Memories

Sometimes it is fun to write a poem about a special memory. Here are some examples of simple memory poems:

> *Lorentza in Monterrey*
> *4 years old*
> *Sitting in a tree*
> *Waiting for my father to come home from work*

> *Koichi in Tokyo*
> *11 years old*
> *Playing baseball after school*
> *Eating junk food before dinner*

> *Letizia in Forte dei Marmi*
> *17 years old*
> *Playing the guitar*
> *Singing with my friends*

> *Abdullah in Jeddah*
> *8 years old*
> *Riding a donkey*
> *Getting water for my family*

Writing Your Memory Poem

A. To write this type of memory poem, think back to a specific time in your childhood. Think about how old you were, where you were, and what you were doing. Use the samples as a guide.

1. On the first line, write your first name and the name of the place where you were.

    _____

2. On the next line, write your age at that time.

    _____

3. On the third line, write exactly what you were doing (using the present progressive tense).

    _____

4. On the last line, give further information about what was going on (using the present progressive tense).

    _____

5. Make any changes that you want to make in your memory poem. Then copy it below.

    _____

    _____

    _____

    _____

B. Write two more memory poems.

_____

_____

_____

_____

_____

_____

_____

_____

C. Choose one of your memory poems and read it to your class.

D. Copy your memory poem on a separate piece of paper.
After your teacher has checked it, paste the poem in your autobiography (p. 106), under the title "My Memory Poem."

Memory Drawing

A. Think of a special memory from your childhood. Do a very simple drawing of that memory on a separate piece of paper.

B. Use the ideas in your drawing to write a paragraph about this memory. Write your paragraph under your drawing. When you are finished, paste both the drawing and the paragraph in your autobiography (p. 107) under the title "A Memory from My Childhood."

On Your Own

A. Make up a story based on this photo of a traffic jam. Imagine that you are in one of the cars. Tell your reader the time and place of your story in the first sentence. Tell what happened in the next few sentences.

_____

_____

_____

_____

_____

_____

B. Exchange paragraphs with a partner. Make sure the sentences are in logical time order.

A. Read the following paragraph. It contains seven mistakes. With a partner, find the seven mistakes and correct them.

> I remember the time my roommate, Ellen, got so mad at me. Was cold that morning, and I borrow a sweater from her. By lunchtime it was warm, so I take the sweater off. I forgot about the sweater and leave it in the cafeteria. When I went back to get it, it was gone. My roommate is furious with I. The sweater was a gift from her old boyfriend. His mother had knit it for her. Ellen was so angry and upset that she doesn't speak to me for a week.

B. Copy your corrected paragraph on the lines below. Then check your work in the Answer Key on page 96.

_____

_____

_____

_____

_____

_____

_____

_____

Your Autobiography

A. Go through your autobiography (pp. 97–107) and make sure it is complete.

B. Revise and illustrate some of the sections if you think it is necessary.

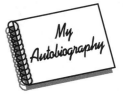

C. Share your autobiography with your classmates.

JUST FOR FUN

Match the holiday with the day or date when it is celebrated in the United States. Then check your answers in the Answer Key on page 96.

HOLIDAY	WHEN CELEBRATED
_____ 1. Memorial Day	a. February 14
_____ 2. Martin Luther King's birthday	b. third Monday in February
_____ 3. Presidents' Day	c. second Monday in October
_____ 4. Labor Day	d. December 25
_____ 5. New Year's Day	e. July 4
_____ 6. Saint Patrick's Day	f. third Monday in January
_____ 7. Columbus Day	g. March 17
_____ 8. Christmas Day	h. fourth Thursday in November
_____ 9. New Year's Eve	i. October 31
_____ 10. Valentine's Day	j. November 11
_____ 11. Independence Day	k. first Monday in September
_____ 12. Thanksgiving	l. December 31
_____ 13. Veteran's Day	m. last Monday in May
_____ 14. Halloween	n. January 1

ANSWER KEY

Chapter 1

You Be the Editor

Five mistakes

> My name is Stanley Stoico. I am 90 years old. I was born in Ravenna, Italy, and lived there until I was 9 years old. Then I moved to New York with my parents and my three older brothers. In my younger years I had many different jobs. I worked hard and saved my money. By 1945 I had saved enough money to start my own retail business. The business was successful, and I retired in 1973. My hobbies are studying the stock market and playing golf. I have seen and done a lot in my long life. I am a lucky and happy man.

Chapter 2

You Be the Editor

Five mistakes

> My cousin's name is Bettina Lee. She is 37 years old. She was born in Chicago, Illinois, but now she lives in Denver, Colorado. She is married and has two children. Bettina is a beautiful ice-skater. She used to skate professionally in ice shows when she was single. Now she teaches ice-skating to young children.

Chapter 3

You Be the Editor

Seven mistakes

> Gary Lesneski is an obstetrician. His work days *are* never typical. He never *knows* what time a baby will decide to be born. Sometimes he has to go to the hospital in the middle of the night. Other *times* he stays at home but *gets* many *phone* calls during the night. Occasionally he sleeps through *an* entire night without any interruptions. Dr. Lesneski likes *his* work. No two days are ever the same.

Chapter 4

Quiz

A. The Five Best Exercises for the Heart and Lungs
1. cross-country skiing
2. running
3. bicycling
4. aerobic dancing
5. swimming

B. Five Exercises That Are Easiest on Your Body
1. swimming
2. walking
3. yoga
4. bicycling
5. cross-country skiing

You Be the Editor

Seven mistakes

There are many ~~benefit~~ *benefits* of exercise. First of all, regular exercise ~~help~~ *helps* people deal with stress. Physical activity also increases your level of energy. People who ~~exercises~~ *exercise* regularly feel less tired than people who ~~does~~ *do* not. A third benefit ~~are~~ *is* that exercise can help prevent memory loss. If you are active when you are young and stay active, ~~You~~ *you* can help prevent some of the problems of aging. For good mental and physical health, experts recommend 20 to 30 minutes of exercise at least three ~~time~~ *times* per week.

Chapter 5

You Be the Editor

Seven mistakes

John Fitzgerald Kennedy was born ~~in~~ *on* May 29, 1917, in Brookline, Massachusetts. ~~She~~ *He* graduated from Harvard University in 1940. From 1941 ~~in~~ *to* 1945, he served in the United States Navy. ~~On~~ *In* 1953, he ~~marries~~ *married* Jacqueline Lee Bouvier in Newport, Rhode Island. He was elected president of the United States in 1960. Kennedy ~~is~~ *was* assassinated three years later ~~in~~ *on* November 22, 1963, in Dallas, Texas.

Chapter 6

You Be the Editor

Seven mistakes

Honolulu is a great place to go for a family vacation because it ~~offer~~ **offers** something for everyone. For example, Waikiki Beach is perfect for anyone who enjoys water sports ~~,~~ **.** It is one of the most famous beaches and surfing areas in the world. The hikers in your family will want to climb Diamond Head. ~~Is~~ **It is** a 760-foot volcanic crater. The shopping ~~in~~ **is** fabulous ~~is~~ **in** Honolulu. Hawaiian arts and crafts ~~is~~ **are** very popular. Some members of your family might enjoy going to a hula show or a luau dinner in the evening. Other examples of ~~populars~~ **popular** activities include the aquarium, the zoo, and the rain forest.

Chapter 7

You Be the Editor

Seven mistakes

The Loch Ness monster is **a** large animal that many people believe lives in a lake in northern Scotland. Hundreds of people say that they have seen the animal. In their descriptions, they say that it is about 30 ~~foot~~ **feet** (9.14 meters) long and 6 feet (1.85 meters) wide. It looks like a dinosaur. They say that it has two ~~fin~~ **fins** like a fish, two ~~hump~~ **humps** like a camel, and **a** long, thin neck. The earliest descriptions of the ~~loch ness~~ **Loch Ness** monster go back to the year A.D. 565.

Chapter 8

You Be the Editor

Seven mistakes

Driving on a wet or slippery road can be ~~danger~~ **dangerous.** If your car ~~start~~ **starts** to skid, ~~this~~ **these** tips may be helpful. ~~Firstofall,~~ **First of all,** slowly take your foot off the gas pedal. ~~Turns~~ **Turn** the steering wheel slowly and only as much as necessary to keep your car on the road. Next, if you have to use your brakes, ~~pumps~~ **pump** them gently up and down. ~~Final,~~ **Finally,** do not try to stop or turn quickly.

Chapter 9

You Be the Editor

Seven mistakes

I remember the time my roommate, Ellen, got so mad at me. ~~Was~~ *It was* cold that morning, and I ~~borrow~~ *borrowed* a sweater from her. By lunchtime it was warm, so I ~~take~~ *took* the sweater off. I forgot about the sweater and ~~leave~~ *left* it in the cafeteria. When I went back to get it, it was gone. My roommate ~~is~~ *was* furious with ~~I~~ *me.* The sweater was a gift from her old boyfriend. His mother had knit it for her. Ellen was so angry and upset that she ~~doesn't~~ *didn't* speak to me for a week.

JUST FOR FUN

Match the holiday with the day or date when it is celebrated in the United States.

	HOLIDAY	WHEN CELEBRATED
_m_	1. Memorial Day	a. February 14
_f_	2. Martin Luther King's birthday	b. third Monday in February
_b_	3. Presidents' Day	c. second Monday in October
_k_	4. Labor Day	d. December 25
_n_	5. New Year's Day	e. July 4
_g_	6. Saint Patrick's Day	f. third Monday in January
_c_	7. Columbus Day	g. March 17
_d_	8. Christmas Day	h. fourth Thursday in November
_l_	9. New Year's Eve	i. October 31
_a_	10. Valentine's Day	j. November 11
_e_	11. Independence Day	k. first Monday in September
_h_	12. Thanksgiving	l. December 31
_j_	13. Veteran's Day	m. last Monday in May
_i_	14. Halloween	n. January 1

My Autobiography

by _____

To Introduce Myself

The Things I Like to Do

My Family Tree

My Family

My Best Friend

My Daily Activities

My Favorite Holiday

My Favorite Hobbies

What I Do to Stay Healthy

What I Look Like

The Way I Am

My Home

My Hometown

My Haiku

My Dream Car

My Finished Story

My Memory Poem

A Memory from My Childhood